More Christn Piano Solos

T0082996

For All Piano Methods

Table of Contents

Book: ISBN 978-1-4234-8364-9
Book/CD: ISBN 978-1-4234-9329-7

HAL•LEONARD®
CORPORATION
7777 W. BLUEMOUND RD. P.O. BOX 13819 MILWAUKEE, WI 53213

Visit Hal Leonard Online at
www.halleonard.com

Santa Claus Is Comin' to Town

Words by Haven Gillespie
Music by J. Fred Coots
Arranged by Phillip Keveren

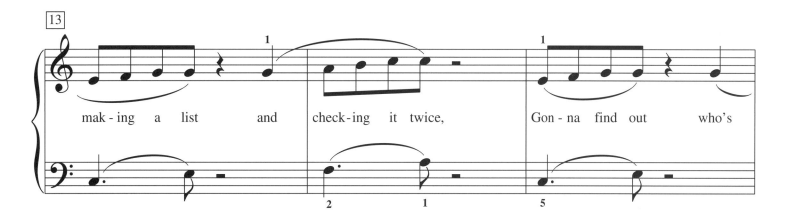

mak - ing a list and check-ing it twice, Gon - na find out who's

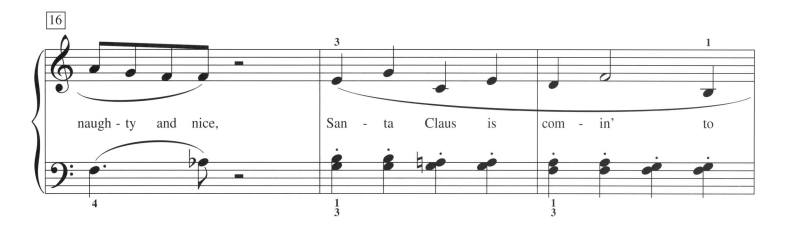

naugh - ty and nice, San - ta Claus is com - in' to

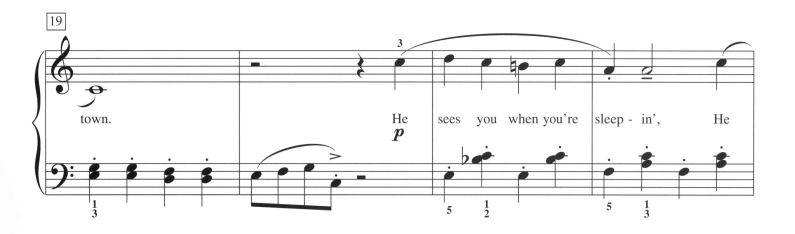

town. He sees you when you're sleep - in', He

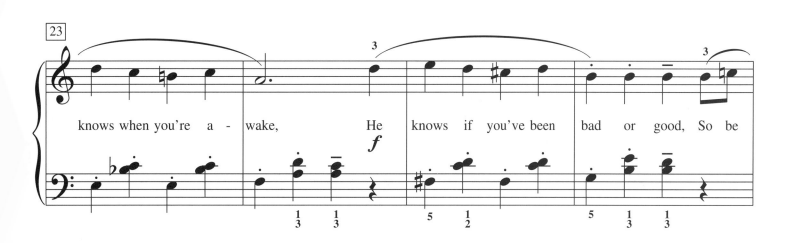

knows when you're a - wake, He knows if you've been bad or good, So be

3

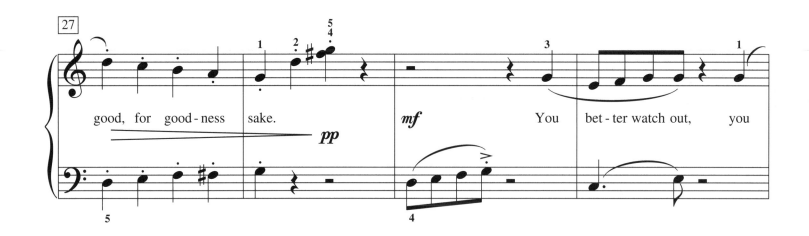

good, for good - ness sake. *pp* *mf* You bet - ter watch out, you

bet - ter not cry, Bet - ter not pout, I'm tell - ing you why:____

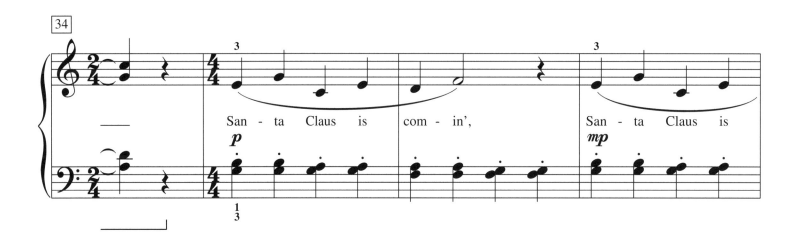

____ San - ta Claus is com - in', San - ta Claus is

p *mp*

com - in', San - ta Claus is com - in' to town!

mf *f*

Wonderful Christmastime

Words and Music by
Paul McCartney
Arranged by Mona Rejino

The mood is right, the spir-it's up,
The par-ty's on, the feel-ing's here

we're here to-night and that's e-nough.
that on-ly comes this time of year.

Sim - ply hav - ing a won - der - ful Christ - mas - time.

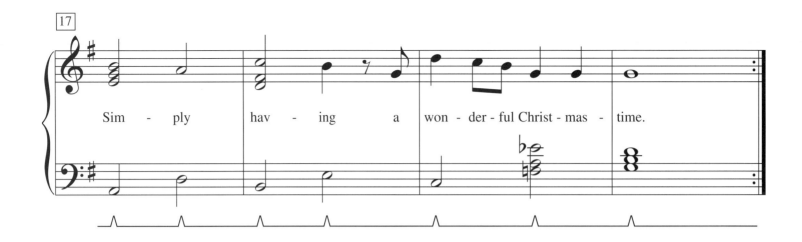

Sim - ply hav - ing a won - der - ful Christ - mas - time.

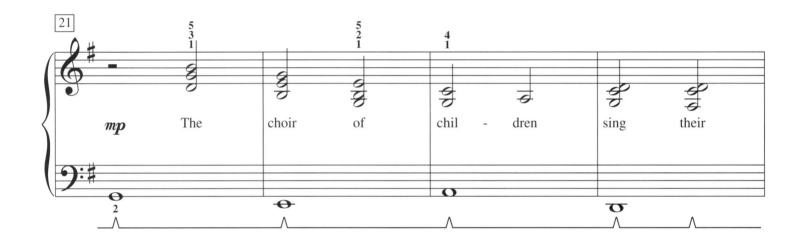

mp

The choir of chil - dren sing their

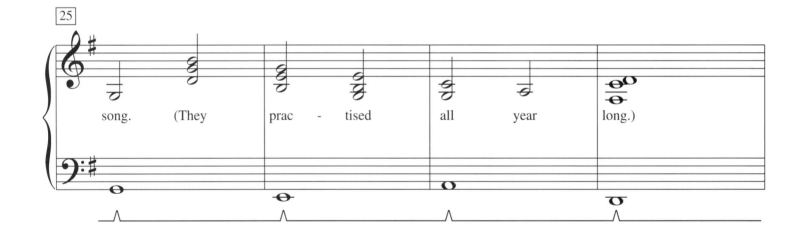

song. (They prac - tised all year long.)

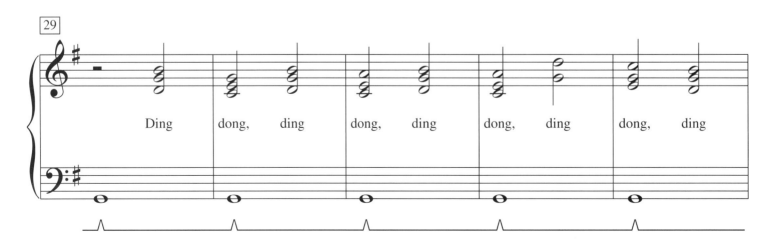

Ding dong, ding dong, ding dong, ding dong, ding

What Child Is This?

Words by William C. Dix
16th Century English Melody
Arranged by Phillip Keveren

Tenderly (♩ = 104)

TRACKS 5/6

What Child is this ___ who,

laid to rest, ___ on Mar - y's lap ___ is

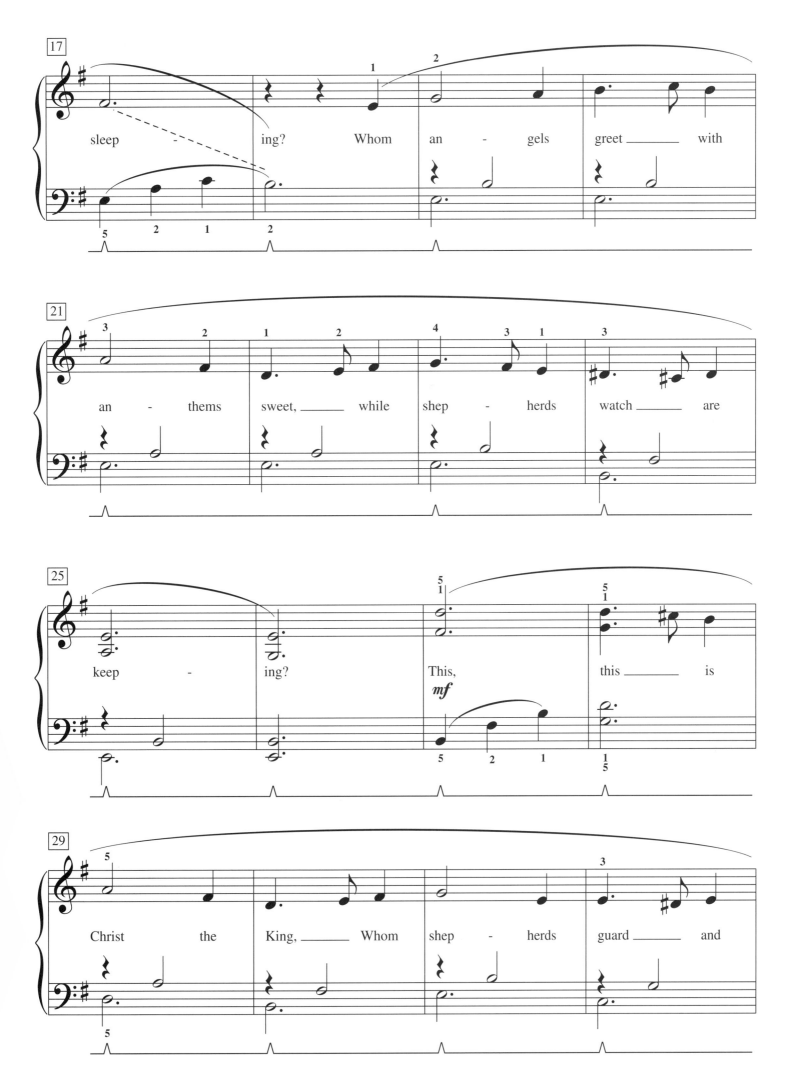

an - gels sing: Haste, haste _____ to
bring Him laud, _____ The Babe, _____ the Son _____ of
Mar - y!

O Come, O Come, Emmanuel

Traditional Latin Text
15th Century French Melody
Arranged by Fred Kern

Moderately (♩ = 100) **TRACKS 7/8**

mp

O

come, O come, Em- man - u - el, and ran - som cap - tive

Is - ra - el, that mourns in lone - ly ex - ile

here un - til the Son of God ___ ap - pear. Re -

f

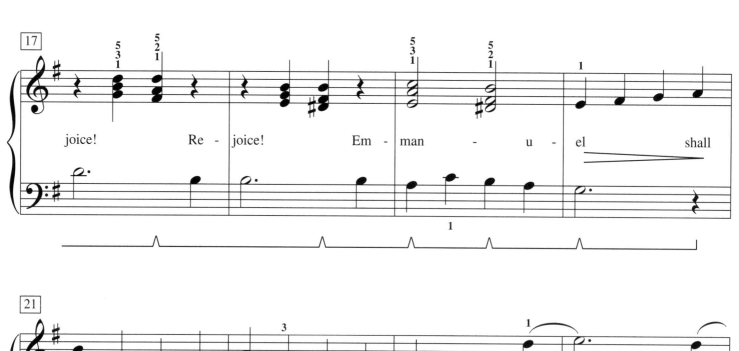

joice! Re - joice! Em - man - u - el shall

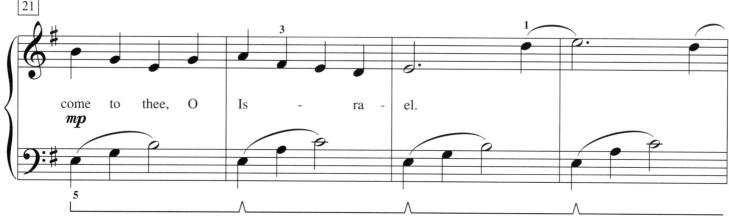

come to thee, O Is - ra - el.
mp

O come, thou wis - dom from _____ on
mp

high, and or - der all things far _____ and nigh; to

us the path of know - ledge show and cause us in her
ways _____ to go. Re - joice! Re - joice! Em -
man - u - el shall come to thee, O Is - ra -
el.

Snowfall

Lyrics by Ruth Thornhill
Music by Claude Thornhill
Arranged by Phillip Keveren

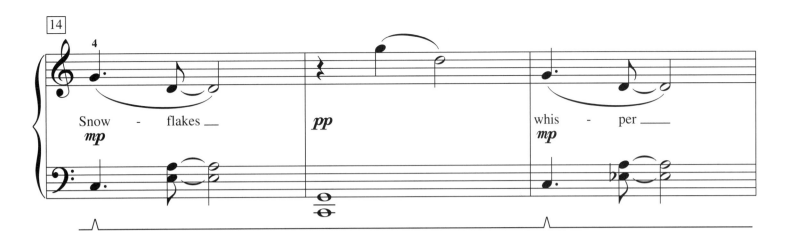

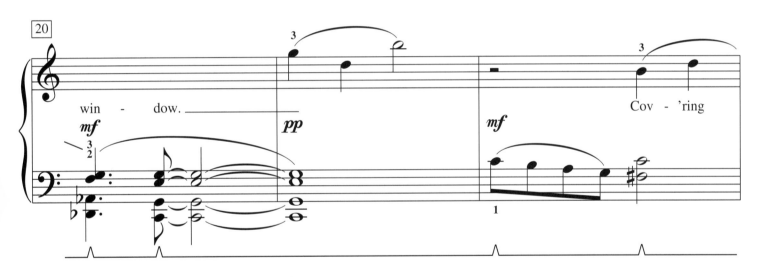

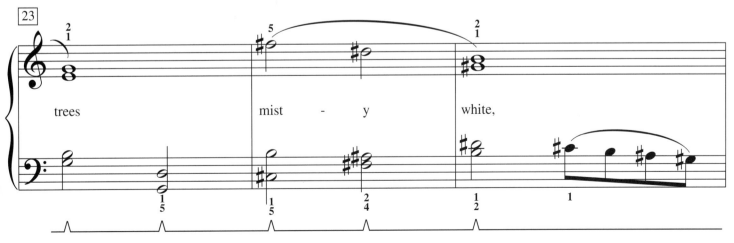

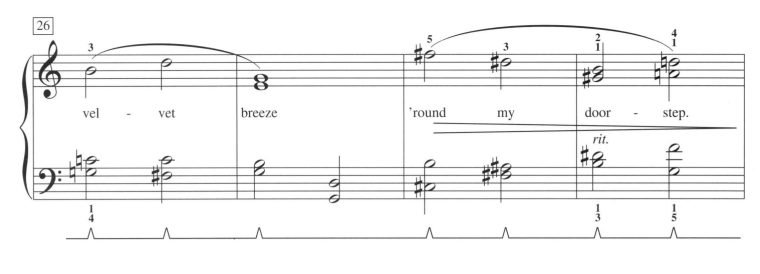

vel - vet   breeze   'round   my   door - step.

rit.

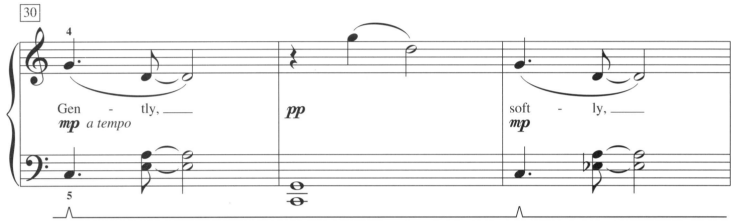

Gen - tly, _____   *pp*   soft - ly, _____

mp a tempo   *mp*

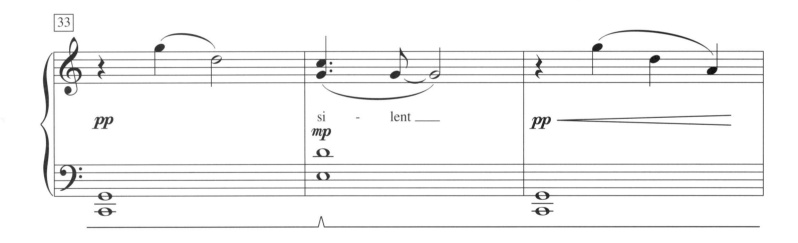

pp   si - lent _____   *pp*

mp

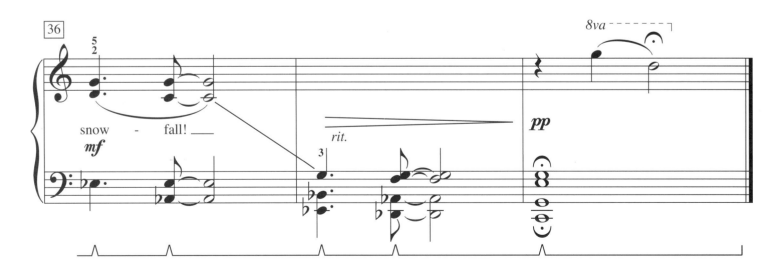

snow - fall! _____   *rit.*   *pp*

mf

It Came Upon the Midnight Clear

Words by Edmund Hamilton Sears
Music by Richard Storrs Willis
Arranged by Fred Kern

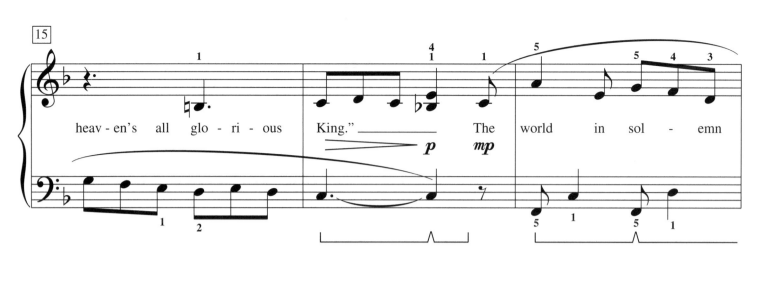

heav-en's all glo-ri-ous King." The world in sol-emn

still-ness lay, to hear the an-gels sing.

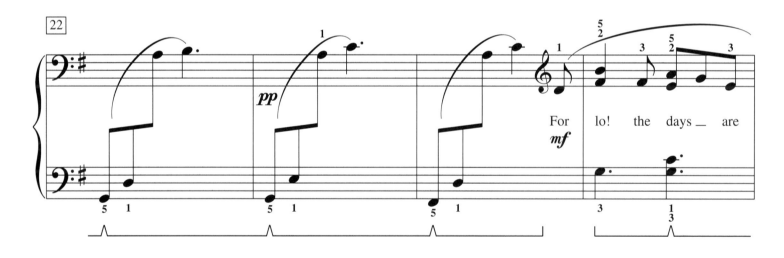

For lo! the days are

hast-'ning on, by proph-et seen of old, when with the ev-er-

18

cir - cling years shall | come the time __ fore - told __ | when peace shall o - ver

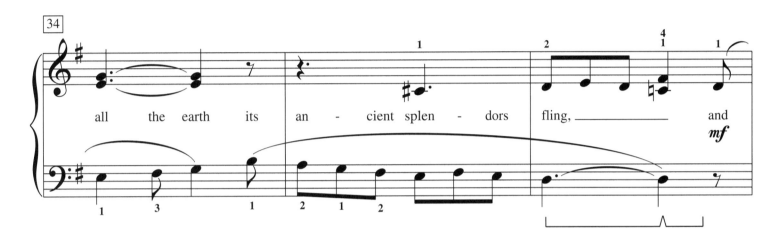

all the earth its an - cient splen - dors fling, _____ and

the whole world __ send | back the song which | now the an - gels

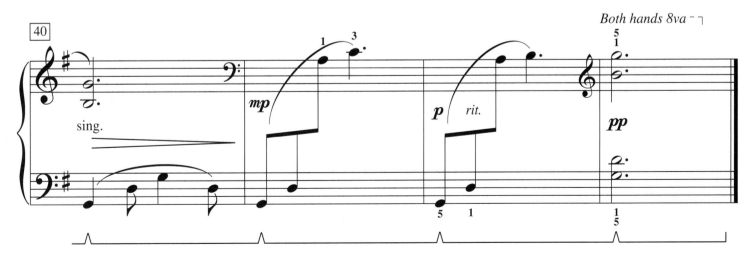

Both hands 8va

sing.

Grandma Got Run Over by a Reindeer

Words and Music by
Randy Brooks
Arranged by Jennifer Linn

as for me and Grand - pa, we be - lieve.

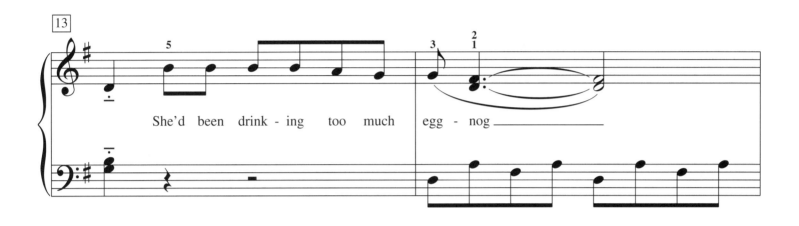

She'd been drink - ing too much egg - nog _____

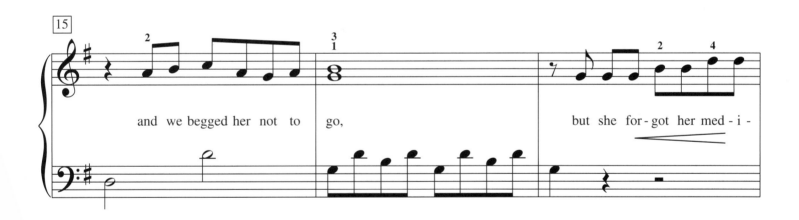

and we begged her not to go, but she for - got her med - i -

ca - tion, _____ and she stag - gered out the door in - to the snow.

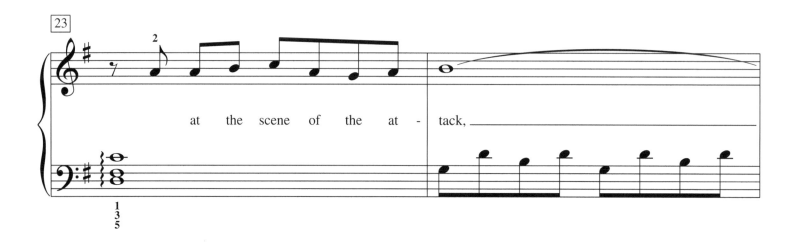

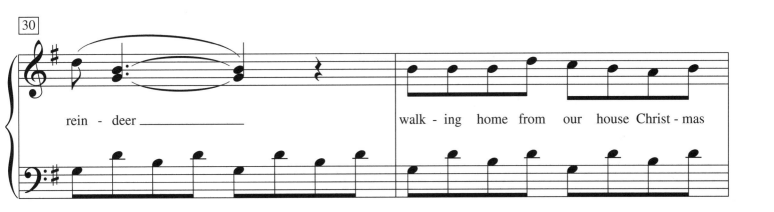

rein - deer _____ walk - ing home from our house Christ - mas

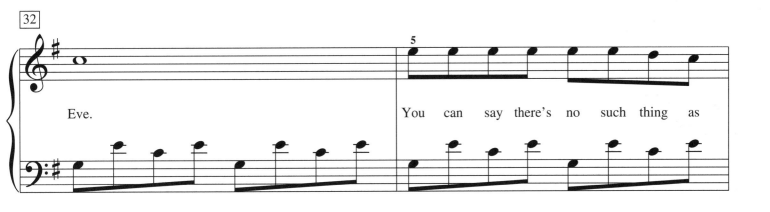

Eve. You can say there's no such thing as

San - ta, _____ but as for me and Grand - pa, we be -

lieve. _____

f

Believe

from Warner Bros. Pictures' THE POLAR EXPRESS

Words and Music by Glen Ballard
and Alan Silvestri
Arranged by Fred Kern

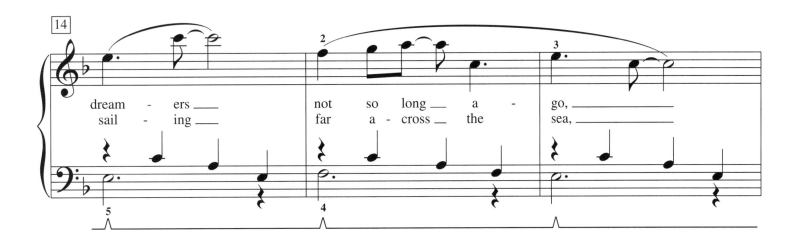

dream - ers ___ not so long ___ a - go, ___
sail - ing ___ far a - cross ___ the sea, ___

but one by one, we ___ all had to grow ___ up.
trust - ing star - light ___ to get where they need to be.

When it seems the mag - ic slipped a - way, we find it all a - gain on Christ - mas
When it seems that we have lost our way, we find our - selves a - gain on Christ - mas

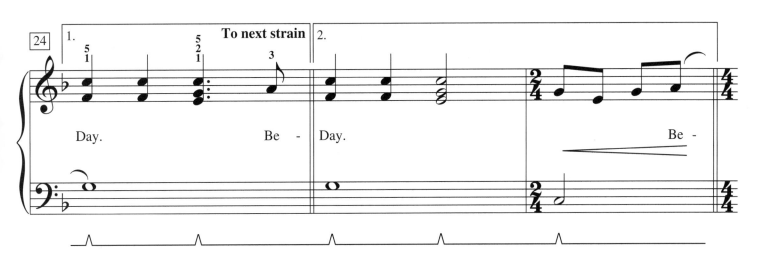

To next strain

1.
Day. Be -

2.
Day. Be -

25

lieve,   if you just be - lieve,

mf

if you just be - lieve.   *p*   Just   be -

lieve,   just be - lieve.

mp

Repeat and Fade

p   *pp*

27

Bring a Torch, Jeanette, Isabella

17th Century French Provençal Carol
Arranged by Carol Klose

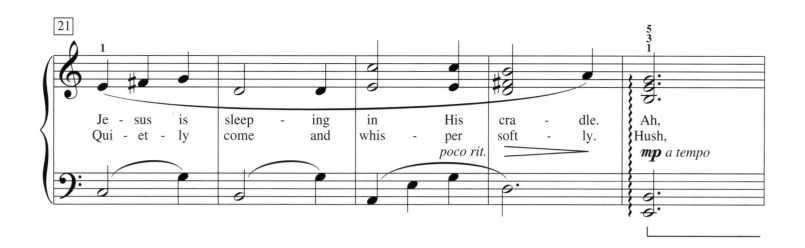

Je - sus is sleep - ing in His cra - dle. Ah,
Qui - et - ly come and whis - per soft - ly. Hush,

poco rit.

mp *a tempo*

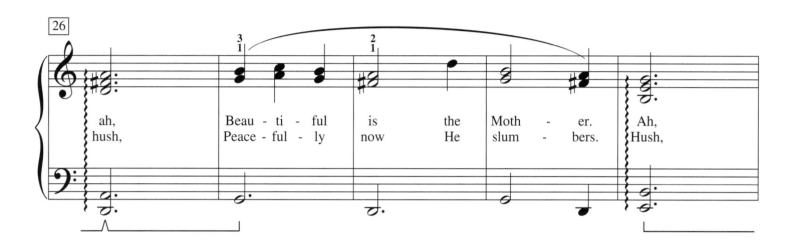

ah, Beau - ti - ful is the Moth - er. Ah,
hush, Peace - ful - ly now He slum - bers. Hush,

1.

ah, Beau - ti - ful is her Son. _____
hush, Peace - ful - ly

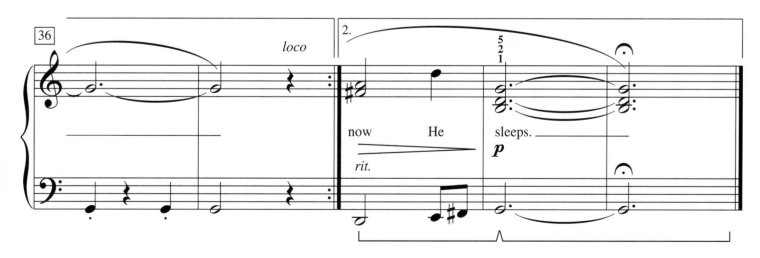

loco

2.

now He sleeps. _____

p

rit.

Lo, How a Rose E'er Blooming

15th Century German Carol
Translated by Theodore Baker
Music from *Alte Catholische Geistliche Kirchengesang*
Arranged by Mona Rejino

Do You Hear What I Hear

Words and Music by Noel Regney
and Gloria Shayne
Arranged by Carol Klose

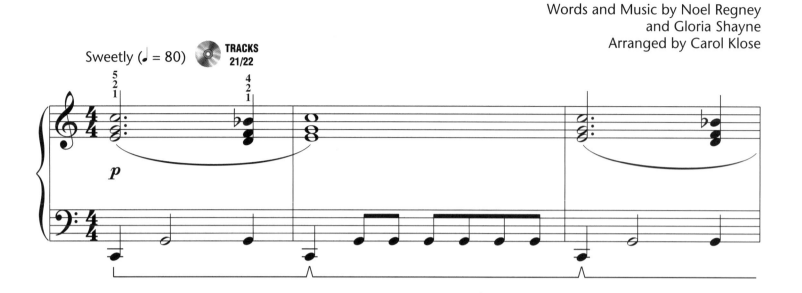

Said the night wind to the lit - tle
lit - tle lamb to the shep - herd

lamb,   "Do you see what I   see?
boy,   "Do you hear what I   hear?

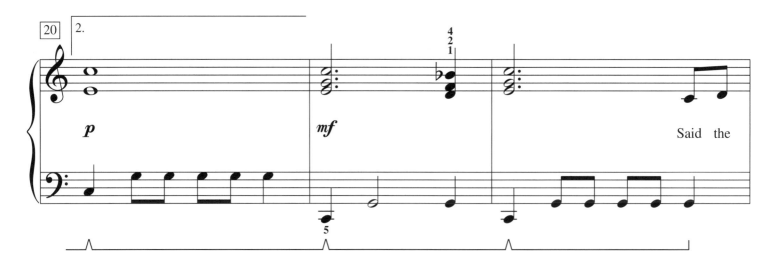

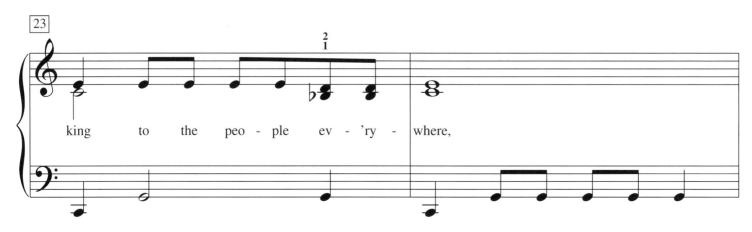

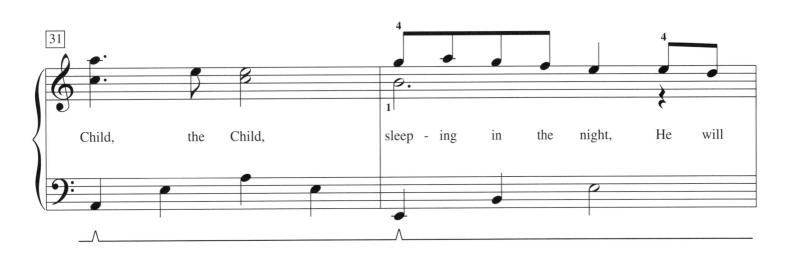

Child,   the Child,   sleep - ing in the night, He will

bring us good - ness and light,   He will bring   us

good - ness   and   light."   *f*

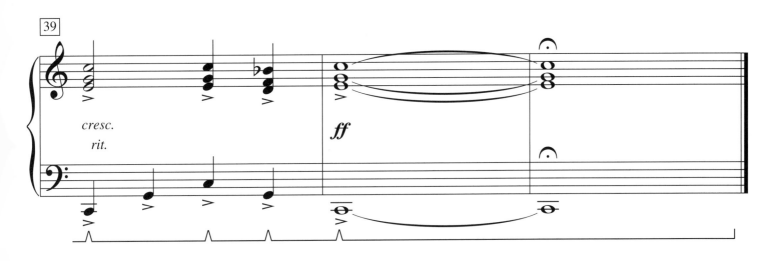

cresc.
rit.   ***ff***

O Holy Night

French Words by Placide Cappeau
English Words by John S. Dwight
Music by Adolphe Adam
Arranged by Fred Kern

Gently, moving (♩. = 56)   TRACKS 23/24

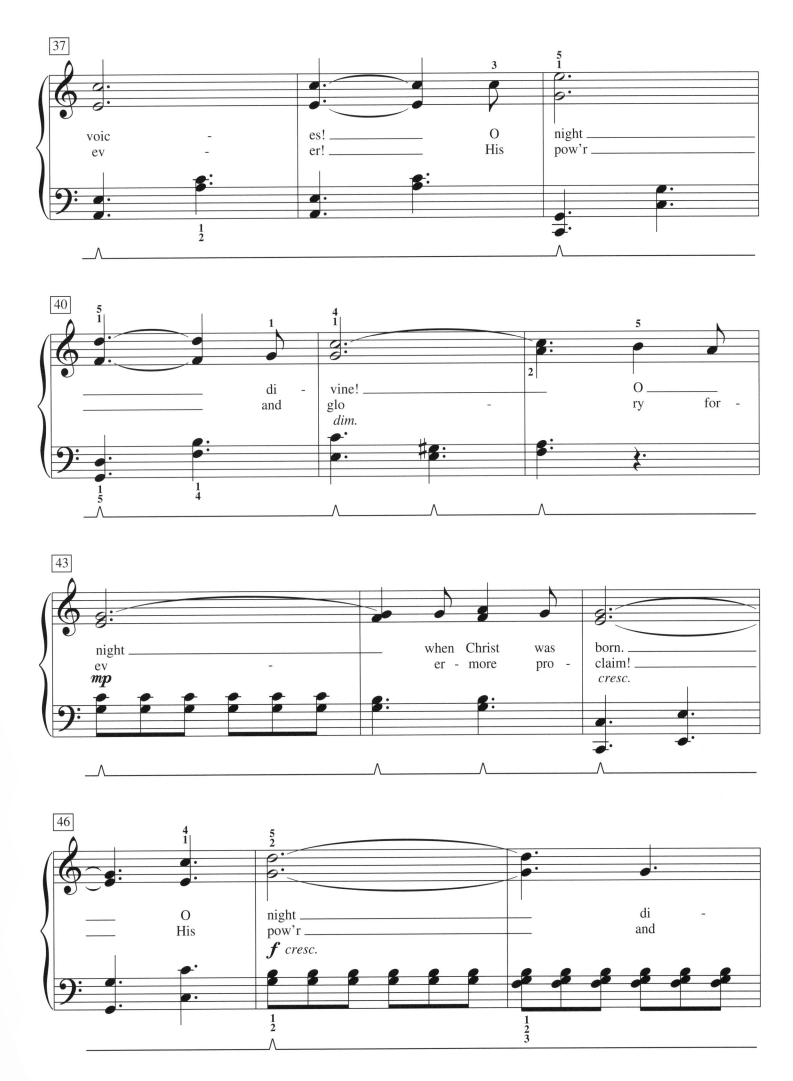